TYRA

This is the first comprehensive exploratı.…
a central theme in the history of political thought. wanc. _
that modern tyranny and statecraft differ fundamentally from the classıca.
understanding. Newell demonstrates a historical shift in emphasis from the
classical thinkers' stress on the virtuous character of rulers and the need for civic
education to the modern emphasis on impersonal institutions and cold-blooded
political method. The turning point is Machiavelli's call for the conquest of
nature. Newell traces the lines of influence from Machiavelli's new science of
politics to the rise of Atlanticist republicanism in England and America, as
well as the totalitarian regimes of the twentieth century and their effects on
the present. By diagnosing the varieties of tyranny from erotic voluptuaries
like Nero, the steely determination of reforming conquerors like Alexander
the Great and Julius Caesar, and modernizing despots such as Napoleon and
Ataturk to the collectivist revolutions of the Jacobins, Bolsheviks, Nazis, and
Khmer Rouge, Newell shows how tyranny is every bit as dangerous to free
democratic societies today as it was in the past.

Waller R. Newell is Professor of Political Science and Philosophy at Carleton
University. He is the author of *The Soul of a Leader: Character, Conviction, and
Ten Lessons in Political Greatness* (2009); *The Code of Man: Love, Courage,
Pride, Family, Country* (2003); *What Is a Man? 3,000 Years of Wisdom on the
Art of Manly Virtue* (2000); and *Ruling Passion: The Erotics of Statecraft in
Platonic Political Philosophy* (2000).